Fishing
with the Birds

Written by Lynette Evans
Photography by Ted Wood

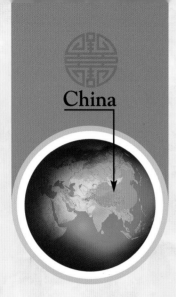

China

Kun Yi lives near the Li River in China. In the early evenings, he goes fishing with his father. Many people use fishing boats, nets, and poles to catch fish, but Kun Yi's father fishes with birds in the old way. By helping his father, Kun Yi learns to respect the ways of the past.

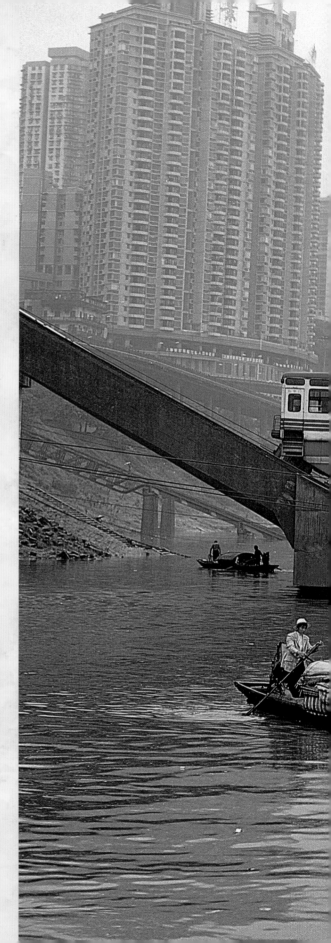

respect to admire and value

Contents

Fishing with the Birds

In the evenings, Kun Yi goes fishing with his dad. They don't go fishing with poles and nets. Instead, they go fishing with birds.

Kun Yi has a favorite fishing bird. Her name is Shiao, which means "little colorful bird."

Shiao is a little
like a pet, but she is
also a worker.
What other animals
live with people
in this way?

Shiao is a cormorant. She has a very
sharp beak, which is good for diving,
and her webbed feet are good for
swimming. She is very good at catching
fish. In Kun Yi's family, Shiao has
a special job to do.

cormorant a web-footed waterbird

Kun Yi lives near the Li River in China. Fishing is a tradition in Kun Yi's family. Long ago, Kun Yi's grandfather fished with cormorants. Now Kun Yi is learning from his father how to fish with birds, too.

tradition an old and special way of doing things

Kun Yi's father knows each bird by name. He tells Kun Yi that he is now old enough to take responsibility for caring for the birds. It is time for Kun Yi to help train them, too. Kun Yi must learn to allow the birds to have a share of the fish. He must never be greedy and take more than his share.

responsibility being trusted with something

Before they go fishing, Kun Yi ties
a piece of grass around Shiao's neck.
The grass does not hurt her. Shiao will dive
and grab a fish with her sharp beak, but
she won't swallow the fish while she has
her grass necklace on.

How do Kun Yi and
his father care for
Shiao and the other
birds that help
them fish?

Kun Yi's dad has a boat made of bamboo.
He uses a long pole to push the boat along
the river. When he finds a good fishing place,
he splashes the water with the pole. Then Shiao
and the other cormorants start diving for fish.
Kun Yi's father explains to his son how this old
way of fishing is kind to the environment.

bamboo   a plant with strong, hollow stems

When Shiao feels the pole under her feet, she grabs hold of it. She is then lifted onto the boat.

When the basket is full, Kun Yi unties the grass necklace. Then Shiao can catch fish and eat until she is full.

Kun Yi helps get the fish out of her mouth and into the basket. Shiao dives in again.

After fishing, it is time to go home. Kun Yi and his brother are hungry for dinner. Can you guess what's cooking?

Hao chi!

Something Fishy

Ingredients:
- one freshly caught fish, cleaned
- one red bell pepper, sliced
- one bunch spring onions, sliced
- sweet and sour sauce

Method:
Fry fish in hot oil in a wok. Add sliced vegetables. Top with sweet and sour sauce.

Yum!

魚 = **Fish**
Yu

More fish are caught in China than anywhere else in the world. Many people fish far out at sea in large boats called *junks*. Others fish on rivers, lakes, or ponds. Some fishing families hardly ever set foot on land.

Children in China begin to use chopsticks as soon as they are old enough to hold them. The Chinese word for chopsticks is *kuaizi,* which means "quick little boys."

Fruit and vegetables are an important part of meals. In China, the way a meal looks is also important. People often carve flowers and leaves out of fruit and vegetables.

 Explore China

China is the third largest country, in area, in the world. It has high mountains, dry deserts, forests, and farmland. Huge rivers twist and turn from the mountains to the sea.

More people live in China than in any other country in the world. The Chinese can trace the stories of their people back in time for more than 3,000 years.

你好 = **How are you?**
Ni   Hao

This is an outdoor vegetable market in the city of Xi'an. The agriculture industry provides nearly all the food needed to feed China's population.

The Great Wall of China was built during the Ming Dynasty (1368–1644). One of the highest parts of the wall is on Mount Badaling, which is near Beijing. Beijing is the capital city of China.

On the Go!

How do many people get around China's crowded cities?
Go to page 16

What is the most important Chinese festival?
Go to page 19

What useful gifts has China given the world?
Go to page 22

RUSSIA

MONGOLIA

Huang (Yellow) River

Beijing

CHINA

NEPAL

Chang (Yangtze) River

Shanghai

INDIA

Li River

Hong Kong

VIETNAM

People and Places

There are many busy, crowded cities in China. Long ago, the emperors who ruled China built big, beautiful palaces in Beijing. Today, Chinese cities are a mixture of old and new, with high-rise buildings, apartments, factories, theaters, and restaurants next to ancient palaces and temples.

People often walk or use bicycles to get around China's crowded cities. Buses and trains are used for longer journeys. Very few people own a car, but they are becoming more popular.

Most people in China live
in the countryside. Farmers
grow crops such as rice, wheat,
and tea. In many places, people
still farm using traditional
methods. Buffalo are often
used to plow the fields.

17

Feasts and Festivals

People all across China take time off to celebrate special days of the year. Each festival has its own customs. Families and friends gather to share food, and there are bright lights and fireworks. There are also races, games, and parades. People dress up and dance in the streets.

What special festivals and feasts does your family celebrate throughout the year?

custom a special way of doing things

New Year is the most important festival in China. People all around the world enjoy taking part in Chinese New Year celebrations.

On the Wild Side

China is the only country where giant pandas are found in the wild. They live in the thick bamboo forests of western China. Bamboo is the only food that giant pandas eat.

There are not many giant pandas left in the wild. Over the years, many bamboo forests have been cleared. Today, the people of China are trying to save the bamboo forests and the giant pandas that live there.

Today there are about 1,600 giant pandas in the wild. This is an increase of 40 percent since they were last counted in the 1980s.

Bamboo plants are really giant grasses that grow as tall as trees. Bamboo forests can be so thick that giant pandas are hard to find and study.

The giant panda grows up to 6 feet tall and weighs between 200 and 300 pounds. Panda cubs usually stay with their mother for more than two years.

Made in China

China has given the world many gifts. The Chinese were the first to invent the compass, paper, and silk cloth. They also invented the wheelbarrow, matches, kites, and fireworks. Today, modern Chinese factories make everything from bicycles to bulldozers, which are sold in many countries around the world.

invent to think of and make something brand new

Calligraphy is the art of beautiful writing. People in China are famous for their calligraphy, which is almost like painting.

People everywhere enjoy flying kites. It is thought that the first kites were made in China 2,000 years ago. Today, kites come in many shapes and sizes.

What Do You Think?

1 Kun Yi helps his father fish for food for his family. What jobs do you do to help your parents?

2 What traditions do you follow in your family? How are these traditions special to you?

How does fishing with birds show responsibility toward the environment?

Index